Where is it?

a wildlife hunt for Kiwi kids

Ned Barraud

pb potton & burton

Where is it ... **in the estuary?**

bar-tailed
godwit

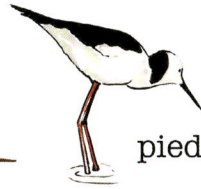

pied stilt

black swan

spur-winged
plover

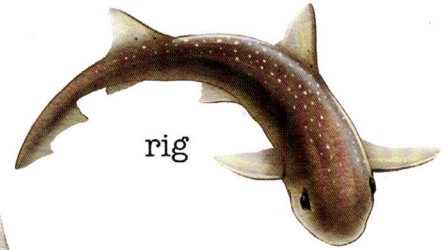

rig

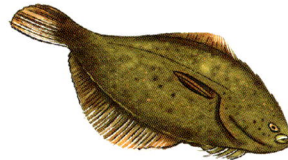

flounder

royal
spoonbill

short-eyed
mud crab

kingfisher

paradise shelducks

little
black shag

cockle

tuatua

yellow-eyed mullet

pipi

banded dotterel

white-faced heron

Where is it ... **in the wetlands**?

kōtuku

spotless crake

inanga

grey duck

dabchick

damselfly

giant kōkopu

green
bell frog

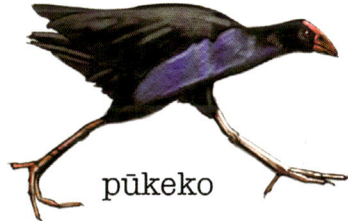
pūkeko

swamp harrier

coot

dragonfly

bittern

fernbird

Where is it ... **in the river**?

giant dragonfly

cockabully

mayfly nymph

welcome swallow

brown trout

kingfisher

little black shag

torrentfish

scaup

rainbow trout

koi carp

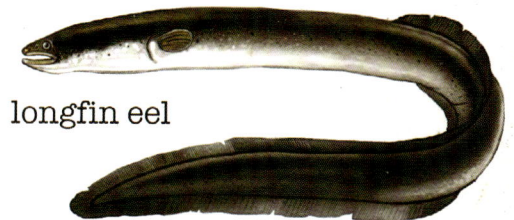

longfin eel

mallard ducks

white-faced heron

dobsonfly

Where is it ... **in the mountains**?

red deer

hare

black-backed gull

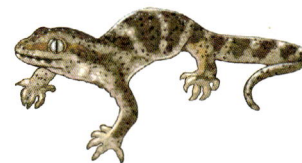

Southern Alps gecko

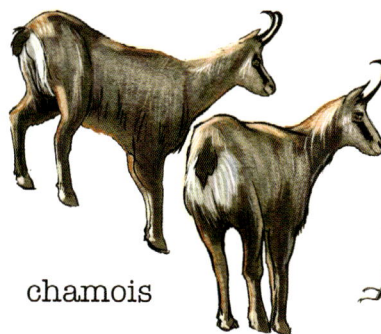

chamois

black cicada

pipit

black mountain ringlet butterfly

grasshopper

rock wren

scree skink

tahr

kea

goat

Where is it ... **on the beach**?

kahawai

katipō

stingray

pied shag

Cook's turban shell

New Zealand sea lion

snapper

black-backed gull

oystercatcher

bluebottle

black-fronted tern

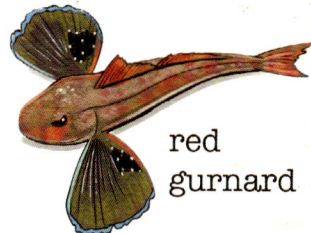
red gurnard

little penguin

paddle crab

scallop shell

ostrich foot shell

red-billed gull

Where is it ...
on the rocky shore?

kina

barnacles

oystercatcher

pāua

periwinkle

fur seal

seahorse

cushion star

purple shore crab

glass shrimp

reef heron

wandering anemone

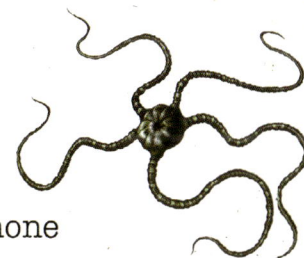
brittle star

chiton

cockabully

black-backed gull

blue mussels

cat's eye snail

Where is it ... **in the deep sea?**

krill

king crab

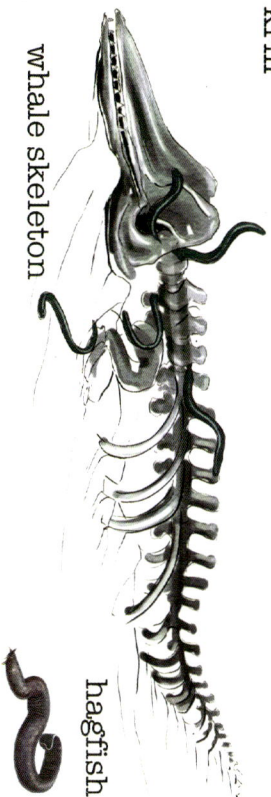
whale skeleton

gulper eel

blobfish

hagfish

humpback anglerfish

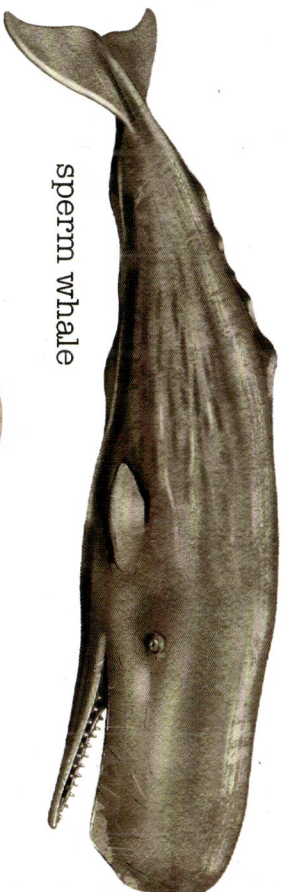
sperm whale

orange roughy

frilled shark

gaint squid

lantern fish

vampire squid

Where is it ... **in the open ocean**?

common dolphin

gannet

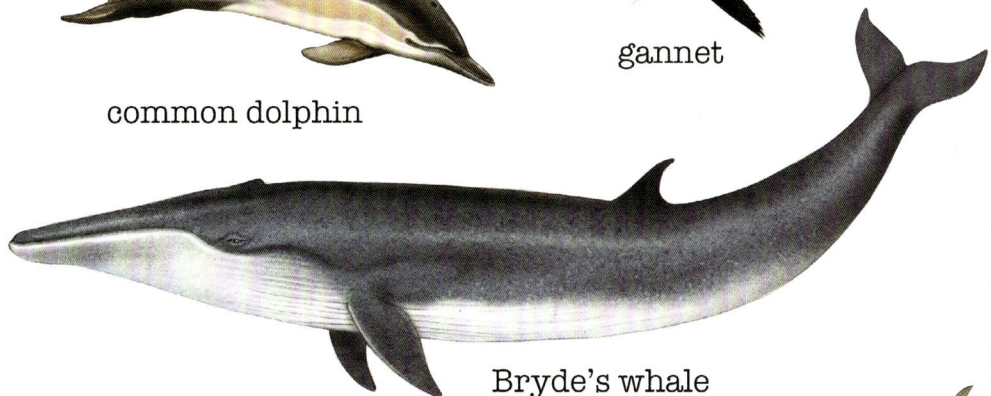

Bryde's whale

mollymawk

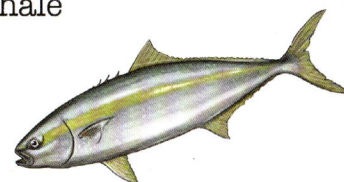

kingfish

orca

fluttering
shearwater

pilchard

leatherback turtle

wandering
albatross

fairy prion

marlin

hammerhead shark

Where is it ... **in the forest**?

fallow deer

stoat

grey warbler

tūī

wasp

kererū

bellbird

pīwakawaka

tomtit

tree wētā

ruru

long-tailed cuckoo

forest gecko

velvet worm

giant land snail

Where is it ... **in the sanctuary**?

giant wētā

kārearea

Hamilton's frog

New Zealand robin

tuatara

rowi

hihi

kōkako

tīeke

whitehead

takahē

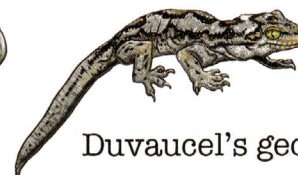
kākā

Duvaucel's gecko

kākāriki

mohua

pāteke

Where is it ...
in the ancient forest?

New Zealand
quail

huia

Haast's eagle

piopio

little
bush moa

laughing owl

long-billed
wren

giant moa

adzebill

Extra information on many of the creatures you have found in this book

Estuary

banded dotterel/tūturiwhatu: This bird keeps very well hidden, especially in the breeding season. But, because it makes its nest in open shingle and sand, it can be easily harmed by rats, cats and even humans by mistake. The 'band' comes from a brown and chestnut-coloured stripe around its breast.

bar-tailed godwit/kuaka: The godwit breeds in western Alaska and flies (migrates) to New Zealand for summertime. The long flight takes 8 or 9 days and covers a distance of over 12,000 kilometres. This is the longest nonstop flight of any bird and it doesn't even stop to snack along the way.

black swan/kakīānau: The black swan was introduced from Australia in the 1860s. There are now about 50,000 black swans living here. It is a large black bird, with red eyes and dark grey legs, and white flight feathers on the edges of its wings. It is a herbivore, which means it eats freshwater plants and even grazes on grass when on land.

cockle/tuangi: Cockles are found just beneath the surface of mudflats and sandflats in low tide. They can burrow and move forward using their 'foot', and they feed on plankton (small, live animals and plants floating in the water).

kingfisher/kōtare: Found in freshwater, estuaries and open country, the kingfisher feeds on crabs, tadpoles and small fish, and even spiders, lizards, mice and small birds. It is often seen perched on power lines, or on rocks or branches near water. The kingfisher uses its sharp beak to tunnel into soft tree trunks or clay banks to build a nest for its young.

flounder/pātiki: The flounder is an extremely flat freshwater fish. The baby sand flounder begins its life with one eye on each side of its head. As it grows into a juvenile, one eye moves to the other side, so it ends up having two eyes on the side facing up.

little black shag/kawaupaka: The smallest of the shag species, it feeds on fish, eels, frogs, tadpoles and insects. Shags need to hang their wings out to dry after diving for food because their feathers are less oily than other birds' feathers. However, it also means they can dive further and stay underwater for longer.

paradise shelduck/pūtangitangi: This duck is endemic to New Zealand, which means it is found nowhere else in the world. Male and female pairs mostly stay close together. The female has a white head and an orange-brown body; the male has a glossy green-black head and dark body. Paradise shelducks mainly eat pasture grasses and clover.

pied stilt/poaka: This black-and-white wader has a slender neck and long legs so it can feed in deep water. It is very clever at distracting predators from its nest by pretending to have a broken leg or wing. The pied stilts feed and roost in large and noisy flocks, especially on South Island riverbeds.

pipi: This shellfish is found buried in sandbanks and is a very common bivalve (meaning it has two shells hinged together). There can be over 1000 pipi per square metre in some areas.

rig/makō: The rig uses its small, flat teeth to crush and eat shellfish and crabs. Rig, or lemon fish as it's also known, is a common fish of choice in fish and chip shops.

royal spoonbill/kotuku ngutupapa: The royal spoonbill is one of six spoonbill species worldwide, and the only one that breeds in New Zealand. It eats mainly fish in freshwater, and shrimps in tidal flats, and other aquatic insects and frogs. It feeds by sweeping its bill from side to side in shallow water.

short-eyed mud crab/pāpaka: A large, strong crab with brownish-grey shell and legs, this mud crab usually sits just outside its tunnel, ready to retreat at any sign of danger.

tuatua: It is like a cockle and pipi, and is also found buried in sand in low tide throughout Aotearoa, however, the hinge of the tuatua shell is more sharply edged than a pipi shell.

white-faced heron/matuku: This is a tall blue-grey bird. It is found at rocky shores and estuary mudflats, as well as near the edges of lakes and on farm ponds. Both the male and female share in raising their young, building the nest together high up in trees and taking turns to incubate (sit on the eggs) and feed the chicks.

yellow-eyed mullet/kātaha: These fish are found in sheltered harbours and estuaries around Aotearoa, usually swimming in large schools. They are often caught by people fishing from wharves.

Wetlands

bittern/matuku hūrepo: This is one of New Zealand's most difficult birds to find. It is a threatened species, and its wetland habitat (home) is often destroyed to create farmland and towns. Males attract females with a deep booming call. You can occasionally see a bittern along wetland edges or flooded paddocks but it will adopt a 'freeze' stance, its bill pointing to the sky when it's caught out in the open.

coot: This black bird, with a white patch on its forehead and bill, can often be seen diving and surfacing with small clumps of weed in its beak, which it feeds on. It will also land and graze on blades of grass.

dabchick/weweia: The dabchick has large, powerful 'lobed' feet (meaning that each unwebbed toe has a stiff flap along both sides). The feet are set far back on its body so it can propel and steer in water. It can dive up to 4 metres, and can hold its breath for around 40 seconds. The adult gives short, chattering calls during breeding season and when alarmed.

damselfly/kēkēwai: The damselfly is a fabulous hunter, catching its prey in mid-air and using its legs like a basket. You can tell the difference between a damselfly and a dragonfly by the wings: damselflies fold them up over their body when they land; dragonflies hold theirs open.

fernbird/mātātā: The fernbird is a small, long-tailed songbird. Being a poor flier, it is more at home hopping around in the wetland vegetation and likes to remain hidden. It easts insects, especially caterpillars, flies, beetles and moths, spiders, and occasionally seeds and fruit.

giant kōkopu: The largest of the kōkopu species, it can grow up to 50 centimetres. It prefers to live in streams with slow, flowing pools shaded with vegetation, while it waits to feed on bugs and insects that fall into the stream from the overhead trees.

green bell frog/poraka: New Zealand's most common frogs are the green bell frog and the southern bell frog, both introduced from Australia around 1870. The female green bell grows to 9 centimetres; the male, 6 centimetres. The female lays thousands of eggs on the water, and they hatch as small, black tadpoles.

grey duck/pārera: The grey duck is in fact a dark-brown duck with a black crown; the face is cream and crossed with two black stripes, and it has greenish-brown legs. It is found in wetlands, and eats mostly seeds and the tips of aquatic plants. Some insects, freshwater snails and worms are also part of its diet.

inanga: This is a small, silvery-white native fish with a slender body. The juvenile inanga is commonly known as whitebait. Eggs are left among the vegetation out of the water and hatch at the next spring tide.

kōtuku/white heron: Rare in New Zealand, with only one breeding population of just 100–120 birds near Ōkārito, South Westland, the kōtuku is highly regarded for its elegant white feathers, long, slender legs and thin, S-shaped neck. It feeds mostly on small fish (such as whitebait), eels, frogs, shrimp, mice and small birds, grabbing its prey with its sharp, dagger-like beak.

pūkeko: The pūkeko is a beautifully multi-coloured bird: its head, chest and throat are a deep blue/violet, its wings and back are black, with white under-tail feathers, a bright red bill, forehead and eyes, but orange legs and feet. It is usually found near sheltered swamps, streams and lagoons.

spotless crake/pūweto: Very shy and rarely seen, the spotless crake forages (hunts for food) in open mud near vegetation, but quickly hides when disturbed. It weaves a cup-shaped nest out of grass and leaves above the water. Because they are so secretive, it is difficult to know how many there are in New Zealand or much about their behaviour.

swamp harrier/kāhu: New Zealand's largest and most common bird of prey, the harrier has an important role in the environment as it feeds on carrion (animals that die on our roads and farms). The swamp harrier is long-legged with big taloned feet and a hooked bill.

River

brown trout/taraute: First introduced into New Zealand in the late 1860s from Britain, brown trout are now the most widespread and common introduced fish in New Zealand waters.

cockabully: These are a familiar sight in New Zealand rock pools but are also found in fresh water. There are many types of cockabully, or triplefins, with the redfin being the most common. They live on the bottom of lakes and rivers and you can usually spot them because of the darting movements they make when they're disturbed.

dobsonfly: This large native insect is found throughout New Zealand's stony riverbeds. As a larva (an immature stage before it is an adult), a male is also called a toe biter because of its large, jagged mouthparts, but actually it is only the female that bites.

giant dragonfly/kapokapowai: This is the largest dragonfly in Aotearoa. A fast-flying, long-bodied insect, it has a yellow and black body and can grow to 9 centimetres long. Its wings are large and transparent (see-through), which spread out sideways when it is resting.

koi carp: This fish is a pest in New Zealand, but native to Asia and Europe. It is brightly coloured, with blotches of black, red, orange, gold and white. Koi carp feed like vacuum cleaners – moving along the bottoms of streams, lakes and rivers, but destroying the aquatic plants as they go.

longfin eel/tuna: Eels migrate up streams as young 'elvers' to find a suitable place to live as an adult. After many years, they return to the Pacific Ocean to breed and then die. The longfin eel is one of the largest eels in the world and it is found only in the rivers and lakes of New Zealand. It is secretive, mainly coming out at night time and preferring places with plenty of cover.

mallard duck: The mallard is the most common New Zealand waterfowl. It is the duck that gathers at local ponds hoping to be fed. Although a strong swimmer, it tends to stay in one place, and it likes to gather in large flocks.

mayfly nymph: Most mayfly nymphs creep around on rocks in lakes, ponds, streams and river edges, eating algae and other small plants. They have three, long tail segments and feathery gills for breathing underwater.

rainbow trout/taraute: Trout were first introduced to New Zealand in the early 1880s. The adult has a silver and dark-green back, covered with many small, black spots, and is light pink along its sides.

scaup/pāpango: A small, black duck, the scaup has legs set far back on its body, and big webbed feet that are perfect for diving for aquatic insects – but it does make them clumsy on land.

torrentfish/panoko: Torrentfish are a common New Zealand fish, well named because they prefer fast-moving water, or torrents. Like whitebait, torrentfish move between freshwater and saltwater to complete their life cycles.

welcome swallow/warou: The welcome swallow is a small, elegant, fast-flying bird. It has a flat head, a forked tail and long, pointed wings. The swallow builds its nest of mud and grass under the roof of farm buildings or other structures such as bridges.

Mountains

black cicada: This small, black New Zealand species is the only cicada in the world that is found in the alpine area (mountains). Like other cicadas, it has a wide head, big eyes, four wings and six small legs.

black mountain ringlet butterfly: This butterfly has the longest life span of any New Zealand butterfly. Because of the high-altitude environment it lives in, where there are long winters and cool summers, the caterpillar can take 2–3 summers to grow to full size.

chamois: Chamois were introduced in 1907 into New Zealand as a gift from the Austrian emperor, Franz Joseph I, in return for specimens of ferns, rare birds and lizards. Chamois are now found throughout the Southern Alps.

goat: Released here in the early days of European settlement to be used for food, fibre and to clear the land, these goats now range from sea level right up to the alpine zone.

grasshopper/māwhitiwhiti: These native grasshoppers are well camouflaged to blend in with the vegetation. They live above the treeline, so they stay frozen under the winter snow, then reanimate (revive) when warmer weather returns.

hare: A hare is bigger than a rabbit and has much longer ears, usually tipped with black. The hare is more suited to alpine regions than rabbits and it relies on its long limbs and large nostrils to escape its predators (animals that hunt other animals for food).

kea: This is the world's only alpine parrot. Kea nest on the ground in natural places such as a gap in a rock or the hollow base of a large tree. They forage (hunt for food) in trees and scrub, looking for fruits, leaves, nectar and seeds. They also dig in rotten logs for huhu grubs, especially in rimu forests.

pipit/pīhoihoi: You might see this small brown-and-white bird hopping about at the beach but also up in the mountains above the snow line. It has a habit of flicking its long tail up and down as it walks (rather than hops).

red deer: Native to Scotland and England, around 250 red deer were released into Aotearoa between 1861 and 1919 as game for hunting. Red deer are the most widespread deer species in New Zealand.

rock wren/pīwauwau:
New Zealand's only true alpine bird, it's a mystery as to how it survives in such a harsh environment all year round. The rock wren bobs along with wing flicks, usually hopping and running rather than flying. It has a high-pitched three-note call and a 'whirring' call.

scree skink/ngārara: The scree skink is a large skink that usually lives in rocky areas in the mountains as well as among boulders and riverbeds. A scree skink will dive into water to avoid being caught.

Southern Alps gecko/ngārara:
This gecko is found mainly on rocky outcrops up to 1800 metres above sea level. You can tell a gecko from a skink by its velvet-like or bumpy skin and because it cannot blink.

tahr: After being released 60 years ago for hunting, tahr spread rapidly and now they are in large herds in parts of the Southern Alps. They damage vegetation and cause soil erosion by their heavy grazing and trampling.

Beach

black-backed gull/karoro:
This bird can be found in countries all around the southern hemisphere, including Australia, South America, and southern Africa. In New Zealand it is very common and can be found from the coast to 1500 metres above the snowline.

black-fronted tern/tara piroe:
The black-fronted tern nests on Canterbury's braided rivers (rivers full of shingle and sediment that build up to make lots of separate channels). The tern has a blue-grey body, wings and a short, forked tail. It is territorial and will dive-bomb intruders close to its colony.

bluebottle/ihumoana:
A type of stinging jellyfish, it has a gas-filled sac that floats on the surface and tentacles that hang underneath. The bluebottle can change the direction of its float and use it to sail with the wind.

Cook's turban shell/kāeo:
This is a large, round, heavy shell. In the past it was used by Māori to manufacture matau, or fishhook.

kahawai: Known as 'the people's fish', it is New Zealand's second most commonly caught species after snapper. Kahawai can be found in harbours, beaches and estuaries throughout the country.

katipō: An endangered species, this native spider spins a tangled web among dune plants or driftwood. Although it has a poisonous bite, katipō bites are actually not very common. The spider is black with a red spot on its back.

little penguin/kororā:
The world's smallest penguin, it was once common on the main islands but is now mainly restricted to offshore islands. It spends its daylight hours at sea.

ostrich foot shell: A large shell with spiral rows of knobs and wavy brown streaks, it is often moved off rocks by waves and washed up on beaches after storms.

oystercatcher/tōrea: This variable oystercatcher has a variety of colours, from completely black to black and white. It uses its strong orange beak to knock open shellfish, but it also feeds on worms and crabs.

paddle crab/pāpaka: During the day, this crab spends most of its time buried in the seabed, with only its eyes and antennae showing. It prefers sandy, sheltered surf beaches. It may give your toe a nip if you happen to stand on it.

pied shag/kāruhiruhi: There are 12 species of shags in New Zealand. In many other countries, shags are called cormorants. This large black-and-white shag is found in coastal areas and usually nests up in trees.

red-billed gull/tarāpunga:
Well known for being noisy and trying to steal a cheeky meal, the red-billed gull is found in large numbers on the seashore. The gull is named for its red bill, but it also has red legs.

red gurnard/kumukumu:
Tucked in beside its brightly coloured wing-like fins, this fish has strange fin rays that help it 'walk' along the sea bottom to find food such as crabs, shrimp and worms.

scallop/tipa: Scallops live in muddy ocean beds and feed on phytoplankton (algae that floats in the water and needs sunlight to grow). Dredging (scooping up) scallops using big buckets has meant there are not so many of them left. The top shell is flat and the bottom half is curved.

sea lion/whakahao: The male sea lion is heavily built with a shaggy lion-like mane. The female is lighter in colour and sleeker. Sea lions prefer sandy beaches, compared to fur seals that are found along the rocky coastline.

snapper/tāmure: A snapper can break open shellfish with its strong jaws. It is a very long-living fish – the oldest recorded was 63 years old.

stingray/whai: This stingray can grow up to 4 metres including its tail. The tail has a serrated (jagged), poisonous spine at the base, used to defend itself but also used on anyone unlucky enough to step on it.

Rocky shore

barnacle/tiotio: When the tide is out, barnacles are shut up tight. As the tide comes in, the shell's plates open and the barnacle waves its feathery legs in the water, brushing tiny pieces of food into its mouth.

blue mussels/pōrohe: Unlike the bigger green-lipped mussel, blue mussels are not grown in 'farms', but can be found attached to rocks between tides. It has a dark blue-black shell.

brittle star/weki huna: Not only can a brittle star regrow parts of its body that drop off but also a small piece can regrow into another whole animal. This incredible ability is called autotomy.

cat's eye/kanohi pūpū: When this snail hides inside its shell, it covers the entrance with a little 'door' called an operculum. Often you can find these green and white doors at the bottom of a rockpool or on the beach.

chiton/papatua: Its eight overlapping shell plates are flexible so the chiton can squeeze into tight crevices and gaps in rocks.

cushion star/pātangaroa: This is a very common sea star in rock pools. Its colours vary from orange-red to blue, yellow and green.

fur seal/hīri: The fur seal was an important food source for early Māori. By the time Europeans arrived, fur seals had almost been hunted out. Europeans also hunted them for their pelts and to use the oil from their blubber. They are now a protected species.

glass shrimp/kōura rangi: Shrimp can live in a wide range of water environments, from freshwater to rock pools where water has evaporated.

kina: Kina is also known as a sea urchin or sea egg. It is covered with long, sharp, brown spines and feeds on seaweed. There are about 70 species in New Zealand, mostly living in deep water.

pāua: With a flattened ear-shaped shell and a row of small holes for breathing, the pāua grips onto rocks, but moves around at night grazing on seaweed. It prefers cooler water and grows larger in the South Island than the North Island.

periwinkle/ngaeti: A turban-shaped mollusk (snail), thousands of these tiny creatures can be found above the high-tide line. They graze on thin trails of seaweed and lichen.

purple shore crab/pāpaka: If you pick up this aggressive crab it may deliver a painful nip. They stay hidden during the day, coming out at night to scavenge and hunt.

reef heron/mātukutuku: Reef herons are extremely rare; the entire New Zealand population is estimated to be between 300 and 500. It is slate-grey in colour, with a long, yellowish bill.

seahorse/kiore moana: Using its tail to grip onto seaweed, the seahorse waits for a passing shrimp, which it can then suck up whole. Its head resembles a horse, but its tail is curled.

Deep sea

frilled shark/mangō: This shark is named for its six pairs of frill-like gills. We can date this shark back to 80 million years ago. It lives its life deep below the surface, and can reach up to 2 metres in length.

giant squid: We know that giant squid are eaten by sperm whales because their enormous parrot-like beaks have been found undigested in whales' stomachs. Giant squid live at extreme depths in freezing water and little is known about their diet or behaviour.

gulper eel: This eel feeds in a similar way to a baleen whale, gulping seafood such as crabs and shrimp or fish from the surrounding water, then squeezing the water out between its teeth and through its gills. Its mouth is larger than its body, and its lower jaw has a pouch, like a pelican.

hagfish: In order to fend off an attacker such as a shark, this fish produces a huge amount of slime from pores on its body to clog up the gills of anything trying to catch or eat it.

humpback anglerfish: Like many deep-sea fish, the female anglerfish has watery flesh and light bones and hangs in the water waiting for passing prey. The female has a lure – an organ with a light at the tip to attract prey. The male is much smaller and has no lure.

king crab/pāpaka: There are many species of king crabs in New Zealand's deep waters; some of them are the largest marine crustaceans (sea creatures with an ekoskeleton, for example, shrimps) ever found, with legs up to 1.3 metres long.

krill/kōura rangi: Very tiny animals with a hard outer shell, krill are sometimes called whale feed because some species of blue whales and humpbacks migrate to the Antarctic from warmer waters every year just to feast on krill.

lanternfish: This is a common deep-sea fish. It gets its name from its ability to produce light, from tiny organs known as photophores – the same ability as a firefly to create a shimmering glow.

orange roughy: First caught in New Zealand in the late 1970s, orange roughy is a slow-growing and long-living fish that does not breed every year.

sperm whale/tohorā: This whale can dive as deep as 2 kilometres while on the hunt for food. Using echolocation (sending out a sound that echoes and returns, to let the whale know the distance to its prey), the sperm whale generates a series of clicks that are the loudest animal-caused noises in the world. An average dive lasts about an hour.

vampire squid: This is neither a squid or an octopus. It is a unique animal that has its own scientific group. It does not suck or drink blood, but instead gets its name from the skin that connects its tentacles that resembles a cape.

Open ocean

Bryde's whale/tohorā: This sleek grey whale looks very similar to the sei whale, also found in New Zealand waters. Unlike other baleen whales that feed on tiny plankton and krill, the Bryde's whale feeds on fish such as pilchard, mackerel and mullet.

common dolphin: Named because they are the most common dolphin found in the Pacific and Atlantic oceans, dolphins in New Zealand can sometimes form pods of thousands travelling together.

fairy prion/tītīwainui: The fairy is the smallest of the prions and one of the most common seabirds in the southern oceans, approximately 95 million individuals. They eat krill and other seafood, which they often peck at while sitting on the water.

fluttering shearwater/pakahā: Shearwaters are long-winged birds that fly just above the sea's surface. Because their nests are burrows that stoats and rats could easily reach, all major breeding sites are now on predator-free offshore islands to protect them.

gannet/tākapu: These gannets are incredible divers, catching fish by plunging high speed into the ocean from heights of up to 20 metres. They breed in dense colonies; one of the largest is at Cape Kidnappers in Hawke's Bay, with around 5000 breeding pairs.

hammerhead shark/mangō: The hammerhead shark is found mostly around the top of the North Island. The hammerhead gives birth to live young, called pups. These are born in shallow bays in litters of 20–50, and they stay with their mum until fully formed.

kingfish/haku: This big, carnivorous (meat-eating) fish with its large mouth is found at the top of the North Island but can also be found at the top of the South Island. It is usually about 1 metre in length and can weigh up to 15 kilograms.

leatherback turtle/honu: These turtles come to New Zealand waters to feed, mainly on jellyfish and small marine invertebrates (animals without a backbone). Because they don't usually come close to land, they are not seen very often.

marlin: The marlin is a large fish. Its upper jaw is like a pointed spear, which it uses to slash through the water to catch small fish.

mollymawk/toroa: A species of albatross found in coastal waters, they are a familiar sight when crossing the Cook Strait on the ferry. They soar above the waves, using their long, narrow wings.

orca/kera wēra: There are an estimated 150–200 orca in Aotearoa. They travel long distances throughout the country's coastal waters. Pods of orca are sometimes spotted around the coastline hunting one of their favourite prey, stingrays.

pilchard/mohimohi: The pilchard has a blue/green top with silver sides and up to 14 black spots along its sides. They swim in vast schools, so pilchards are preyed upon by many creatures, including other fish, seabirds and sea mammals.

wandering albatross/toroa: This is one of the world's greatest travellers, 'wandering' an average of 120,000 kilometres in a year. It is also one of the largest of New Zealand's marine birds, with a wingspan of up to 3 metres.

Forest

fallow deer: Introduced from Europe in 1860, they are known for their paddle-shaped antlers, and for having the biggest range of colours of all deer species, from white to various shades of brown through to black.

giant land snail: Also known as powelliphanta snails, they mainly feed on earthworms. The largest land snails in the world, they can measure about 9 centimetres across and weigh 90 grams. Some of the largest ones are found in Kahurangi National Park.

gray warbler/riroriro: The warbler has a distinctive call, but it can be hard to spot, as it flits about looking for insects in the tree tops.

kererū/wood pigeon: You often hear the 'swoosh swoosh' of kererū wings before you see the actual bird. It eats larger fruit, such as karaka berries, which other birds can't eat. This makes them very important at spreading seed through a forest.

long-tailed cuckoo/koekoeā: You'd be lucky to spot one of these birds in the forest as it hides very well. It is a migratory bird, which means it spends spring and summer in New Zealand to breed, then returns to the Pacific Islands in winter. The female lays its one egg into the nests of either a whitehead, brown creeper or yellowhead, leaving them to raise its chick.

pīwakawaka/fantail: A small, friendly, insect-eating bird, it isn't afraid to come up close to people, swooping and looping to catch insects on the wing. The secret to their success is being able to produce many young, which helps keep the population growing.

ruru/morepork: The morepork is New Zealand's only surviving native owl. A similar species can be found in Australia called a boobook. You can hear the morepork's two-part call start up in the evenings. Early settlers named it more-pork because that's how they thought its call sounded.

stoat/toriura: Introduced in 1879 in New Zealand to control rabbits, the stoat has had a terrible impact on native bird species. The stoat is bigger than a weasel but smaller than a ferret.

tomtit/miromiro: There are five subspecies of tomtit, one of each found on the North, South, Chatham, Snares and Auckland islands. Clear away some leaf litter in the forest and one of these little birds may appear, looking for small insects.

tree wētā: If you listen at night, you may hear a tree wētā rubbing its hind legs against pegs on its body. This is called stridating. The male tree wētā has a huge head with big fierce mandibles (jaws). It battles other males for females.

tūī: This energetic bird is also a great singer, with a wide range of melodies but also strange grunts, coughs and wheezes. It is easily recognised by the little white tuft under its chin. It is common in most parts of the country except Canterbury.

velvet worm/ngāokeoke: This is a living fossil, which has existed, unchanged, for over 500 million years. It has a strange way of catching its insect prey by squirting two jets of sticky glue-like fluid. It then injects saliva that turns its prey's insides into a soup, which it sucks out.

wasp: During the summer months, some beech forests are often abuzz with German wasps. In New Zealand they eat huge amounts of honeydew. Honeydew is produced by an insect on tree trunks and is an important food for native birds, bats, insects and lizards.

Sanctuary

Duvaucel's gecko/ngārara: This is New Zealand's largest gecko. It can grow up to 30 centimetres in length. It lives in forest and scrub and is mainly nocturnal (feeds at night), foraging both on the ground and in trees, and its favourite meal is wētā.

giant wētā/wētāpunga: There are over 70 species of wētā in New Zealand, including 11 different giant wētā. A wētāpunga can weigh up to 35 grams, which is heavier than a house sparrow.

Hamilton's frog: One of four unique native frogs, it is unlike any other frogs in the world because they don't become tadpoles. The embryo develops inside an egg, and then hatches as an almost fully formed frog.

hihi/stichbird: Until the 1980s, hihi were only found on one island in the world, Little Barrier Island, in the Hauraki Gulf. Since then new populations have been successfully established in other North Island sanctuaries, both on the mainland and on offshore islands.

kākā: These large parrots live in the forest, and their harsh, loud call is often heard long before they are spotted. Though they are found throughout New Zealand, they are not common, except when pests are controlled. For example, they are often seen in Wellington city where they have spread from Zealandia Wildlife Sanctuary.

kākāriki: Because of its bright green feathers, 'kakariki' is a good name for this parrot because it is also the Māori word for the colour green.

kārearea/New Zealand falcon: Well known for their speed and ability to dive-bomb and catch small birds in the air, kārearea can be spectacular to watch. They are also very protective of their nests and will not hesitate to attack people who get too close.

kōkako: Kōkako are from an ancient family of birds called wattlebirds. The fleshy purple patches on either side of its head are called wattles. Kōkako are poor fliers; they prefer hopping from tree to tree on their powerful legs.

mohua/yellowhead: The mohua is a small songbird. It is closely related to the whitehead. It lives in family groups high in the canopy of native trees, in the South Island.

New Zealand robin/toutouwai: There are both North Island and South Island species of robin, both found in forest and scrub land. They are often friendly and trusting, and will come within a few metres of you, hopping along the forest floor on their long, spindly legs.

pāteke/brown teal: The pāteke is a rare bird and big efforts are being made to increase the numbers of them. It is a small, chubby duck with white rings around its eyes.

rowi/Ōkārito brown kiwi: One of the rarest of all kiwi, rowi are only found around Ōkārito on the West Coast of the South Island and on a few offshore island sanctuaries.

takahē: These are the largest living, flightless birds in New Zealand. They are part of the rail family of birds, which includes their close relative the pūkeko. Takahē were once considered to be extinct until they were rediscovered in 1948 in a remote Fiordland valley.

tīeke/saddleback: Tīeke came very close to extinction. By the 1960s there were only tiny numbers surviving on some remote islands, but they were saved by transferring the remaining birds to other island sanctuaries, and since then the population of tīeke has slowly started to rise.

tuatara: The tuatara's closest relative is an extinct group of reptiles that were around at the same time as the dinosaurs. Tuatara do not have external ears like lizards do; and they enjoy cooler weather, while lizards like it warm. Tuatara are also nocturnal (come out at night).

whitehead/pōpokatea: Whitehead can be the most abundant forest birds on pest-free offshore islands like Kāpiti and Little Barrier. They live in noisy flocks of up to eight birds and prefer hopping to flying, moving quickly through the treetops when foraging, often hanging upside down.

Ancient forest

adzebill: The size of its deadly looking bill suggests that the adzebill was probably a predator, possibly eating lizards, tuatara and smaller ground birds like the New Zealand quail. It was extinct shortly after the arrival of Māori.

giant moa: The female giant moa weighed 250 kilograms, three times the weight of the male, and she could stretch to a height of 3.6 metres. It was one of the largest birds to have ever walked the earth.

Haast's eagle/pouakai: This eagle had a 3-metre wingspan and weighed up to 13 kilograms. Swooping down from the treetops at 80 kilometres an hour, it could hit a moa with terrible force and deliver very deep wounds with its talons. The Haast's eagle disappeared once the moa started dying out.

huia: The last confirmed sighting of a huia was in 1907. They were hunted for museums and their tail feathers used for hat decorations. For Māori, wearing huia tail feathers was seen as a very high honour and worn by important people only.

laughing owl/whēkau: Also known as the white-faced owl, the laughing owl was about twice the size of a morepork. It was still around when European settlers arrived in New Zealand, but became extinct by about 1914.

little bush moa: This was the smallest species of moa, standing at only 1.3 metres tall. Because it was much more common, it was probably the last moa species to become extinct.

long-billed wren: This wren probably became extinct shortly after Māori settlement. It would have been easy prey for the kiore, the Pacific rat, because it didn't fly and it built its nest on the ground.

New Zealand quail/koreke: This was the only native bird from the pheasant and quail family and the first bird species to become extinct. They were also described as tame, bold and unafraid of humans.

piopio/native thrush: The piopio was described as New Zealand's rarest bird species by the late 1880s.

I live up in the hills of Karori, Wellington, with my wife and three children. I studied art at Victoria University and have since illustrated many children's books and journals, including seven non-fiction titles in Potton & Burton's highly successful Explore and Discover series, as well as *Animals of Aotearoa*, with author Gillian Candler. I have also written and illustrated *New Zealand's Backyard Beasts*, *Moonman*, *Watch out for the Weka*, *Tohorā: the southern right whale*, *Rockpools: a Guide for Kiwi Kids* and *What Happened to the Moa*.

Ned Barraud

First published in 2020 by Potton & Burton
319 Hardy Street, PO Box 221 Nelson
New Zealand

pottonandburton.co.nz

© Ned Barraud

ISBN 978 1 98 855021 3

Printed in China by Midas Printing
International Ltd